Contents

INTRODUCTION

Biodynamics is truly a 'holistic' approach to gardening. It encompasses the principals of organic gardening while taking into consideration the basic cycles of nature. The goal is to restore and maintain balance and of the earth and its ecosystems. The father of biodynamic gardening, Rudolph Steiner, laid the groundwork for this new approach in 1924.

A primary focus of biodynamics is the health and vitality of the soil, which has been depleted over the years by modern agriculture and the use of synthetic fertilizers, pesticides and herbicides. When the ecosystem of the soil is in balance, plants grow large and healthy and produce an abundance of vitamin-rich food. Compost is used extensively, but not always in the traditional manner. Biodynamics incorporates the use of raw compost materials. After digging a deep hole, raw compost material is added in layers alternating with fresh manure. These layers can be heaped up to about 2' above the ground. The seed or plant is then planted. As the plant grows, it has its own supply of rich compost. Incredible results such as tomato plants as large as 12' high by 10' round that produce 2000 tomatoes per plant have been reported. With that kind of result you don't need a large garden!

Biodynamic gardening includes a number of other practices. Among them is working with the biodynamic calendar, the Stella Natura. Biodynamic gardeners time their ground preparation, cultivation, planting and harvesting to be in harmony with the rhythms of the sun, moon and stars in order to enhance the health, vitality and success of their crops.

Biodiversity is another key element of biodynamic gardening. Cover crops, crop rotation, companion planting and non-genetically modified seeds all work together to draw beneficial insects and maintain crop and soil health. All of these practices work together to produce healthy foods that are filled with valuable trace minerals which are often missing from commercial produce.

Pest control, fertilization and soil revitalization are enhanced by specially-formulated Biodynamic Preparations. These unique concoctions, consisting of extracts of plants, minerals or manures, are applied at specific times of the year, usually in small, yet highly potent rates. Some are applied directly to the soil or compost while others are applied directly to the leaves of actively growing plants.

The Basics of Biodynamic Gardening
Biodynamics is both a philosophy and a method of agriculture developed by Rudolph Steiner, a researcher who saw a connection between science, nature, universal laws and spiritual concerns. The agricultural principals at work in biodynamics help people work with nature in order to grow healthier food with minimal environmental impact.

Biodynamic gardening shares certain principles and techniques with organic gardening, such as keeping the soil chemical-free, using compost, raised beds, crop rotation, and companion planting. But biodynamics includes much more. Biodynamic gardening takes the organic garden to the next level and if you are already an organic gardener, incorporating the principles of biodynamics will be simple and beneficial.

Biodynamic gardening first focuses on soil health and the integration of different plants and animals. One of the ways biodynamic gardening differs from other techniques is that it encourages people to take the time to understand their crops and livestock. A key part of the biodynamic philosophy is to know what each individual plant and animal needs to thrive, and then to give it to them. What crops are the best for your pastured livestock to graze on? How much room does each animal need to enjoy optimum health? What nutrient does each plant species require? Is there enough of that nutrient in your soil? Are there companion plants that can strengthen the health of your main crops? These are a few questions biodynamic farmers will ask before jumping into a project.

Basics of Biodynamic Gardening, homesteading, homestead

Composting is essential to the biodynamic farm. The compost pile, when filled with manures and organic waste, creates humus. When humus is spread on the field, it stabilizes nitrogen in the soil, which is crucial to crop health. Composting also means nothing on the farm is wasted. A healthy compost pile will have food scraps, animal manure, and paper products. Vermicomposting, or vermiculture, is another method of composting that gives you more bang for your buck. Not only are you composting scraps, but you are growing your own worms. Not only can these worms increase the yield of your garden, selling them to other gardeners or fishermen can also add to your farm income.

Another technique biodynamics employs for soil health is plant diversity. Unlike monoculture gardening in which only one type of crop is planted, depleting the soil, crop mixing allows plants to support each other. If one plant depletes the soil of a certain nutrient, its neighboring plant releases that same nutrient back into the soil.

Crop rotation and pastured livestock are also an important part of the biodynamic farm. Rotating crops from field to field, raising pastured livestock as well as making use of cover crops and green manures encourages healthy soil, controls weeds, and reduces parasites.

There are several other ways to fight weeds organically. Remember, the most important focus of a biodynamic garden is the soil. Raised beds are effective at reducing weeds, but raised bed gardening is not always an option. One interesting homeopathic method that is successful against weeds is to pile up the weeds you have removed from your planting area and burn them. Collect the ash and sprinkle back over the soil.

A successful biodynamic farm will be a self-supporting, or closed loop, system. A closed-loop system is on in which nothing needs to be brought in, or taken out, of the farm. The waste from one part of the farm becomes energy for another part. When you feed your livestock food you have grown and then their manure naturally fertilizes your garden, you are participating in a closed-loop system. Another way you can work towards a self-supporting system is to collect and save the seeds from your garden. It is a very simple skill to learn that results in stronger and healthier plants that are acclimated to your specific growing conditions.

Biodynamic gardening utilizes biological controls, which occur naturally in chemical-free gardens. Biological control is the use of living organisms, from bats to beneficial insects, to combat unwanted pests. The best way to protect beneficial insects is to stay away from toxic sprays or dusts. You can encourage beneficial animals and insects by providing appropriate habitat and food sources. Hang some bat houses and birdhouses. Leave some weeds in your garden as an alternate food source and shelter. Fill a large bowl with stones and water so small beneficials can drink without drowning. Add plants to your landscape, such as yarrow, dill, and catnip, that are good food sources for adult beneficials.

Biodynamic gardeners also use planetary influences, such as moon phases and zodiac signs, to determine the best time for specific gardening tasks. While this may seem unscientific today, gardening by the moon has been practiced for thousands of years by our ancestors, and science has recently validated the practice, noting that plants respond to the same gravitational pull that affects tides.

Lunar planting is influenced by two factors: the lunar phase and the astrological signs of the zodiac. The lunar phase is what controls the amount of moisture in the soil. Moisture in the soil is at its peak at the time of the new and full moon. The moon causes the moisture to rise in the earth. This encourages seed germination and growth. Each astrological sign corresponds with the elements of water, earth, fire, and air. Each plant has a preference for which sign it is planted in. The path of the moon is divided into twelve sections of 30 degrees. Each section takes its name from the constellation. When you hear "the moon is in Virgo," this simply means the moon is in the same part of the sky as the constellation Virgo.

The moon has four phases. Each phase of the moon lasts about seven days. The first two phases are during the waxing, or increasing light, between the new and full moon. The third and fourth phases are after the full moon, when the light is waning, or decreasing. During the new moon, the lunar gravity pulls water up, causing the seeds to swell and burst. The rising moisture and increasing moonlight during this phase creates balanced root and leaf growth. This is the ideal time to plant above-ground annual crops that produce their seeds outside the fruit, such as spinach, lettuce, celery, broccoli, cabbage, cauliflower, and grain crops. Cucumbers are an exception as they produce their seeds inside their fruit but do well when planted in the new moon phase.

During the second phase, the gravitational pull is less but the moonlight is still strong. This is good for creating strong leaf growth. It is generally considered a good time for planting, especially two days before the full moon. Plant above-ground annuals that form their seeds inside the fruit, such as beans, melons, peas, peppers, squash, and tomatoes. It is also recommended that you mow your lawn in the first and second phase of the moon to increase growth.

After the full moon, the moon begins to wane. The energy of the moon is drawing down. The gravitational pull is very strong, creating more moisture in the soil, but the moonlight is decreasing. This puts more energy into the roots. This is the phase for planting root crops, including beets, carrots, turnips, onions, and potatoes. It is also when you should plant your perennials, biennials, and bulbs. Transplanting is done at this time because of the active root growth. Pruning is also something to do in this phase, in the sign of Scorpio.

The fourth phase is considered a resting period due to the decreased gravitational pull and moonlight. This is the best time to cultivate and to harvest. If you did not transplant or prune during the third phase, it is fine to do that now. Mow your lawn in the third or fourth phase of the moon in order to retard growth.

Just as each phase of the moon is preferred for specific jobs, each astrological sign provides optimal conditions for certain tasks. Match the correct astrological sign with the correct phase of the moon to come up with the ideal time to complete each job.

Things Worth knowing About Biodynamic Farming

- How it all started

The phenomenon we now identify as the organic movement arose in the early twentieth century as agriculture started to become more industrialised and synthetic fertiliser was introduced. Biodynamic farming was born from a series of agricultural lectures in 1924 given by Austrian philosopher and social reformer, Rudolf Steiner (1861 – 1925). He had been invited to a Silesian farm estate by a group of farmers concerned about the negative impact of nitrogen fertiliser on soil quality. Drawing on traditional farming practices and his own "spiritual science" which aimed to bring scientific rigour to spirituality, Steiner suggested a set of practices and principles for sustainable agriculture. He urged his followers to test his ideas and, thanks to this approach, biodynamic farming developed through collaborative research, observation and hands-on farming practice.

- The philosophy behind it

Rudolf Steiner developed Anthroposophy ('anthropo' meaning human, and 'sophia' meaning wisdom), a philosophy based on the premise that all beings can develop their inner potential and access a spiritual world. This philosophy has inspired an education system (Waldorf and Steiner schools), a therapeutic approach for people with learning difficulties (for example, the Camphill Communities), anthroposophic medicine, eurythmy (an expressive art movement) and biodynamic farming.

- Demeter – the first eco-label

Named after the Greek goddess of the harvest, the orange Demeter label is the international logo used for certified biodynamic products. Founded in 1928, Demeter is the world's first ecological food and farming trademark. Used in over 60 countries, Demeter certification verifies that biodynamic products meet international standards in the production and processing of sustainable food. Regulated in the UK by the Biodynamic Agriculture Association (BDA), Demeter's biodynamic standards build on EU organic standards.

- Differences between organic and biodynamic

A UK farmer wishing to be certified for Demeter (biodynamic) accreditation must comply with EU organic regulations requiring a two-year conversion period. For biodynamic certification, Demeter standards require an additional year of conversion to include using eight mineral and plant-based preparations to activate soil life and plant growth on the land. Although there is a large body of observational evidence from farmers showing that biodynamic methods improve soil condition and plant health, more scientific research is needed. However, the long-term DOK field trials by FiBL (Forschungsinstitut für Biologischen Landbau) compared biodynamic (D for Demeter), organic (O) and conventional (K for 'konventionell') cropping systems suggests biodynamic practices are effective. In the biodynamic system, soil organic matter (humus) content remained stable for the first 21 years of the trial while it declined in all other systems.

- Biodynamic preparations for soil and plants

The highly-diluted biodynamic preparations are stirred for an hour to create a vortex and counter-vortex to oxygenate and disperse the active ingredients, then sprinkled or sprayed over soil or plants.

Two preparations, Cow Horn Manure (BD 500) and Horn Silica (BD 501) primarily prepare the fields while the remaining six 'preps' treat compost. Used to enhance soil biology, Horn Manure (BD 500) is made from the fresh manure of pasture-fed cows. Collected in the autumn, it is placed in a cow's horn and buried for six months. When dug-up again, the cow pat has transformed from smelly lumps to a peaty brown-black crumble. Horn Silica preparation (BD 501) is used for plant health. Made from finely-ground quartz (a common stone or sand) and mixed to a paste, Horn Silica is buried in a cow's horn in spring and dug-up in the autumn. Stored in a glass jar on a sunny window sill, it is diluted in miniscule quantities and sprayed as a fine mist on growing plants in the morning.

Just as 1g of rich soil has a billion microorganisms, a biodynamic spray will have microscopic amounts of bacteria and fungi. On one hand it is quantitative, and on other hand it is energetic that is, the quality which goes beyond the physical body. But you do not need to believe in this for biodynamic methods to work.

- Have you ever wondered why cows have horns

This question, posed by Steiner, led to practical evaluation of horns and animal health and the banning of dehorning under Demeter standards. Horns play a vital role in the animal's health. There is a highly developed flow of blood to and from the horns, which appears to improve digestion and metabolism. Horns are also considered health indicators. If a cow's horn smells strongly, I know there is something wrong with her. A cow's horns confer social status, and ensures a cow has more body space.

- Cow dung and soil quality

Biodynamic farmers believe that cattle produce high-quality manure essential for soil health. It is helpful to have cow dung in compost heaps, even in small amounts, to help fermentation and fertility. The biodynamic preparation, Cow Pat Pit (or barrel preparation) can be added to the compost heap as a starter as well as being sprayed on the farmland and garden. It contains cow

manure and the compost preparations and is
recommended for those converting to biodynamic
agriculture. Add a pinch to a bucket of water, stir for
about 20 minutes, then spray, preferably in the autumn.

- Compost is king

Biodynamic farming aims to create healthy soil using
compost and crop and grazing rotations. Uniquely, it
treats the compost heap with medicinal plant-based
preparations (BD 502-507) to encourage the microbial
life needed for soil fertility (and which is suppressed by
chemical fertiliser). The purpose of the compost
preparations is to bring about a harmonious
decomposition process. Biodynamic preparations enable
the composted matter to stabilise and fix the nitrogen
which is volatile. Their effect is to hold the
decomposition process in a disciplined way to prevent
nitrogen loss. If a compost heap gets too hot, it loses
ammonia, a nitrogenous substance. That's like money
dropping out of your back pocket.

- Is biodynamic vegan

While the diluted preparations are mineral, plant and manure-based, some use animal parts as 'sheaths' to hold and help activate the ingredients. For instance, BD 506 consists of dandelion flowers wrapped in a cow's mesentery, the membrane covering the intestines. The parts come from healthy animals which have either been slaughtered for meat or old age. Steiner himself was a vegetarian, and biodynamic farming practice has the highest animal welfare at its heart.

- Planting by the moon, stars and planets

Whilst traditional farming has long used lunar almanacs, the biodynamic calendar also includes constellations and planetary alignments. Inspired by Steiner, the biodynamic calendar, now in its 57th year, was developed by German farmer, Maria Thun (1922 – 2012) who experimented with planetary effects on planting, sowing and harvesting. Now produced by her son, Matthias Thun, the biodynamic calendar can be adapted for particular hemispheres. Although it is not mandatory for Demeter certification, the biodynamic calendar is used by farmers and gardeners.

One of the best ways to learn more about biodynamic growing is to join a local biodynamic group, visit local biodynamic farms or a Camphill Community.

Guide To Upgrading From Organic To Biodynamic Methods

The organic movement has come a long way in recent years and nowadays organically grown fruit and vegetables are almost mainstream.

Permaculture is also understood by more and more people and is spreading world-wide. Yet Biodynamic growing methods together with the 'brand name' of Demeter has some way to go before having the same popular understanding, and some of the myths are dispelled.

So rather than explaining the biodynamic theories based on Rudolph Steiners' lectures, here are some practical tips on how to 'step up' from being an organic gardener to becoming a biodynamic gardener. Hopefully by applying these theories in practice, you can experience these methods.

Biodynamic gardening can allow you to form a better spiritual and physical connection with your garden.

This is achieved by:

- Growing your crops close to nature's rhythms
- Closely observing your garden or the land
- Witnessing an increase in vitality of your soil and plants through application of biodynamic preparations
- Sowing, planting, hoeing, and harvesting in harmony with nature, using the phases of the moon and planets.

What You Need To Upgrade From Organic To Biodynamic

One of the first things you need to try to increase is the vitality of your soil. As an organic gardener you already know that applying chemical fertilizers has a detrimental effect on your soil in the long term. At this stage you may already be using plant based fertilizers (green manures, fertilizers made of nettles, comfrey) or animal manures .

Biodynamic growers enhance soil vitality by applying biodynamic preparations to the land and by also adding compost preparations either to the compost heap or to use as 'teas' to apply to crops and the land. These preparations are applied in very small (homeopathic) quantities and are available from the BDAA. They come with full instructions and there is enough literature around to go deeper into explaining why certain plants are chosen for preparations and why they are stored in an unusual way.

Spring is a good time to use the 'Horn Manure' preparation (made with cow manure stored in a cow horn over winter underground). After stirring a small quantity of cow manure preparation for an hour you apply it to your plot by hand before you start planting.

Spring is also a good time to start a new compost heap and you can add compost preparations such as Yarrow, chamomile, nettle, dandelion, oak bark and valerian, when you have enough material. Again, guidelines and instructions come with the preparations. The nettle preparation is quite easy to make yourself and I have included instructions at the end.

When you are ready to sow and plant, bear in mind that open pollinated seeds are important. All biodynamic seeds are organic, open pollinated and grown on biodynamic farms and land. These types of seeds can be used for seed saving and swapping and plant diversity alive and they will have evolved to suit your local climate and soil conditions.

Biodynamic gardeners and growers see things holistically. For them, harmony and balance comes from sowing the seed, watching the plant go through different cycles in an archetypical way, producing flowers and by collecting seeds again after pollination.

So the biodynamic gardener (who is part of that cycle of life) accurately plans activities in order to best take advantage of various cycles of the moon, planets, stars and sun. You can use various aids (such as lunar gardening calendars) but you will also learn a lot through observation. The biodynamic planting calendars take notice of waxing and waning moon cycles, which are quite easy to observe.

Less obvious is the ascending and descending of the moon's path, which changes once a month from a lower arc to a bigger one. This is just like the sun changing its path in the sky from low in winter to high in summer (as seen from earth in the northern hemisphere). The calendar can assist you in choosing the optimum times to sow, plant, harvest and tend to crops but don't look at it as a dogmatic regime that you have to follow under all circumstances. There are always alternatives if you have missed the optimal time. Practical tips on using biodynamic methods for preparing your beds

After having applied the horn manure preparation in spring, hoe when the moon is waxing and in Leo, (which will bring all weed seeds in the ground to germinate) and then hoe again when the moon is waning and in Capricorn. This will remove the unwanted weed seedlings. To make your very own nettle preparation, dig an area in your garden or allotment deep enough to hold a huge amount of fresh stinging nettles. Cut the nettles in June/July and cover with topsoil. Now you have to wait for a whole year before opening your marked area where you will find a much smaller amount of nettle compost.

The moon is responsible for the tides and is also the ruler of all liquid elements and their movement in the soil, plants and in our bodies. Hence the moons position in the sky will affect the absorption of water and nutrients of plants and you should bear in mind which direction these energies and fluids go when planting and pruning and when you harvest your crops for storage.

Biodynamic Preparations
Different types of preparations and their usage

The horn silica preparation is very finely ground crystal quartz. It is dynamised in water for an hour before spraying and has the effect of giving harmony to the plant by promoting leaf, flower and fruit development.

The horn manure preparation works on plant root development, plant form and its vitality, promotes plant growth, the soil micro-life which is active in the humus fraction and the Ego component of our cultivated plants. The one hour stirring rounds out the 500 making process and it becomes active as it is spread on the land.

Before the horn manure and horn silica preparations are spread, the small amounts necessary for a given area are stirred for an hour in water. This dynamised water is sprayed on the soil and the plants and works in a fashion similar to homoeopathic medicines – as an energiser rather than an addition of matter.

The compost preparations have the task of promoting humus development by drawing in ordering forces from the cosmos. They also promote soil life which is responsible for breaking down all organic materials, and in connection with the mineral clay substances build up the clay-humus complex in the soil. They do this by combining the elements of dead organic materials, soil, soil life and water into vital humus. The cow pat pit (cow pat compost) shows their capacities clearly in its final form.

The compost preparations consist of herbs such as chamomile, nettle, oak bark, yarrow or valerian, most of which are filled into particular animal organs, hung in the summer sun or placed in the soil for some months where they collect cosmic forces during this time. If the animal sheath is omitted or replaced by a plant form during production of the preparation, the resulting preparation does not fulfil the requirements.

Organic Pest Control

Starting a garden comes with its fair share of joys and pains. Along with the fun of gardening comes the difficulty of dealing with hungry bugs that are looking to devour your garden. Fortunately, by understanding how to leverage Mother Nature, you can implement a full pest control strategy in your garden, without toxic chemicals.

Yellow-necked caterpillars defoliating a blueberry bush. If the caterpillars are localized to one or several bushes, hand removal or pruning is sufficient to control the population.

Natural Predators

By introducing good bugs like ladybugs and lacewings into your garden's ecosystem, you will be able to keep the bad bug population down. These bugs act as a twenty-four hour security force, patrolling your garden for menacing pests that seek to destroy your wonderful plant life. You can attract these natural predators to your garden by planting insectary plants or purchasing them.

Companion Planting with Insectary Plants

These are the plants that attract beneficial insects (natural predators) and should comprise 5-10% of your garden in order to provide ongoing support for the beneficial insects in your garden. These plants provide proper food and shelter for the insects that you want to have in your garden. Keeping the beneficial insects happy means they will stay longer and patrol your garden more effectively over a period of time.

Row Covers

In addition to using natural predators, row covers provide great protection from pests, as well as harsh weather. These are fairly simple to install and provide all of the proper nutrients to your garden through the porous material, while keeping out pests. They even provide frost protection during winter months, if you get a heavy-weighted cover. The covers come in various weights depending on your needs and how much protection you want from the elements.

Applying Diatomaceous Earth

Food-grade diatomaceous earth is beneficial and 100% safe for your garden, but dangerous to pests as it punctures their exoskeletons causing dehydration and death. This is an affordable and effective way to organically manage pests in your garden. Since diatomaceous earth loses its effectiveness when wet, re-apply after rainfall.

Managing Fruit Trees With Biodynamic Methods In Your Organic Orchard

Managing fruit trees is a task most backyard gardeners and hobby farmers take on. It can be very rewarding and it is also filled with many challenges of learning, like all food growing. I have found working with biodynamic methods to support organic management of our fruit trees to be very effective and wanted to share some insights.

Managing fruit trees is a fine balance between focusing on growth and quality. Differentiation is another way of expressing quality. It relates to tree and leaf structure, flowering and ripening process, nutrient take up and nutritive qualities of fruits. Managing growth and quality organically requires a range of tactics and these are different for each fruit tree crop.

To really excel in managing fruit trees, you need to observe the life processes of fruit tree crops over long periods of time and be highly objective and active in how you manage them. So the first principle that evolves here for the small scale grower is to limit the variety of crops you grow as this makes it easier to focus. Biodynamic practices, I feel, are ideal in managing the interplay between growth and quality (differentiation) of all fruit trees.

Root and leaf management

Healthy soil is vital for your fruit trees, to strengthen the earthy element of your soil so that it is buzzing with life. Use the following practices:

Apply BD horn manure twice per year around the base and drip line. This will help with the root zone and stimulate stronger leaf growth. Apply under an earth planetary sign. When your plant is young, the growth aspects become more important so extra applications of horn manure to support a healthy root zone will assist. Once the tree is established, get into the twice per year routine and avoid flowering time.

Use compost in your planting hole and once per year around the tree base when in its leafing stage. It is important this is made with biodynamic compost preparations as this balances nutrients and stimulates life processes. You can combine BD horn manure and BD compost preparation in one brew by using the combined soil preparation from BAA

Have living mulch around the base of trees, normally a nitrogen fixing plant such as clover, lucerne, cow pea and let it regrow. BD horn manure will support its growth

Apply biodynamic tree paste once per year after the tree is pruned and do it on an earth sign. This has a big impact on plant vitality, leaf and root growth.

Apply liquid manure around your trees. I prefer BD seaweed and fish emulsion with the BD compost preparations included. This well balanced brew should be OK to apply at most times during the tree cycle, but limit applications to no more than 6 per year.

Flower and fruit management

Apply BD horn silica at the end of leafing stage when it is expected to commence flowering. Once the fruit is reaching a size close to harvest, apply BD horn silica again as this makes a big difference to the flavour and nutritive qualities of the fruit. The BD horn silica helps with the form of the plant, its flowering and fruiting processes and its nutritive qualities, so you can see it has a strong connection to plant differentiation or quality. Apply BD horn silica on a flower (air) planetary sign when the tree is in its flowering stage and on a fire (fruit) planetary sign when you are about to harvest. Harvest your fruit on a fire (fruit) sign as this will enhance nutritive qualities and storage life.

Pest and disease management

For persistent insects, birds and animals use biodynamic peppers which very effectively deter these creatures from turning your trees into their permanent home

Yearly applications of biodynamic tree paste after you have pruned and if you see the plant vitality being pounded by disease or insect attack, apply tree paste will quickly bring the tree back into a healthy state by enhancing its life force

Apply BD horn silica and BD 508 equisetum to assist with photosynthesis in the plant and reduce the impact of moulds. Apply close to the full moon to get best results.

Be sure your orchard space has sufficient sun, is well drained and you supply enough moisture but not too much

Other tactics
Balance of life and biodiversity – Be sure to create habitats for beneficial insects and bird species that do not decimate your crops. This would include: bee hives, bird boxes, border areas around your orchard with berry bushes and herbs to create habitats. I also find that putting out the BD horn manure is a great way to very efficiently manage soil and plant vitality over your whole space, so your orchard does not become such a target for pests.

Choosing ideal cultivars – If you can find a fruit tree nursery that propagates only with organic methods, patronise them. Buy quality, you will be with the tree for a long time and it will reward you well if you look after it appropriately.

The Biodynamic Sowing and Planting Calendar
We are dependent on both the sun and the moon for life on earth, and since time began, both have held a profoundly symbolic importance for mankind. The influences of the Moon's gravitational pull on the seasons and plant growth (as well as animal and human behaviour) has been documented since ancient times. Biodynamics acknowledges these and other subtle cosmic forces, and works with them throughout the growing cycle. This is what is meant when people say 'planting by the moon'.

By using the moon as a guide in our growing, we're attempting to stimulate the latent promise that each crop has to offer. Sometimes we have to compromise because of more immediate constraints of time and weather, but over the years we've noticed that the closer we work with these subtle rhythms of the cosmos, the better these results.

How does the biodynamic calendar work

Each month the moon moves through all twelve constellations of the zodiac in turn. This is referred to as the moon's sidereal cycle and forms the basis of the biodynamic calendar. Although the waxing and waning (synodic) cycle is the most well known lunar rhythm, it plays a small part in this calendar.

Since ancient times the twelve zodiac constellations have been associated with the each of the four elements: earth, water, air and light. Three constellations are connected to each element, and each element is related to a part of the plant: thus, Earth – root; water – leaf; air – flower; fire – fruit.

For example, for sowing or harvesting carrots an earth – root day should be chosen; for lettuce – a water – leaf day; for beans and apples – a fire – fruit day; and for cut flowers and broccoli – an air – flower day. The influences have most effect when the soil is disturbed and /or when the biodynamic preparations have been used. Choosing suitable times for cultivation, as well as for sowing and harvesting, is therefore important.

Principle and Advantages

In order to establish a system that brings into balance all factors which maintain life, the following areas are considered:

Substance and energy

Life is more than just chemicals; it depends on the interaction of matter and energies. For example, plants need light and warmth as well as earth and water to grow. The interaction of substance and energy forms a balanced system. We live not only from substance, but also from energy, and so we need to eat food which will provide the energy. Only plants which have grown in a balanced soil can give us energy (through trace minerals, enzymes, growth hormones) as well as substance.

To produce healthy, vital plants, one must concentrate mainly on the structure and the life of the soil: the nutrients, the trace elements, the microorganisms, the worms and other animals present in the soil. But primarily, the soil is a living system of connections and relationships. If the soil is balanced in its life forces, the plants growing in it will be stronger, healthier, and higher in quality. No chemicals necessary. In terms of structure, the soil should be crumbly, friable, well aerated and deep in order to be fertile.

Organic matter

In order to create this balanced, living soil, what is required is skilful use of organic matter. This is done by building compost heaps and using the Biodynamic compost preparations.

Humus

This mysterious, magical substance supports life and is the carrier of all that the plants need to grow. It holds the fertility of the soil in a stable way, and retains water. Humus is completely digested crude organic matter: rich, dark, and moist with a fresh odour. This is the base for building up the soil and fostering its formation should be the first priority when converting to Biodynamic farming.

Cow manure

This is a very special substance given to us by the holy animal Cow which is essential for healthy soil life. Cow dung is special because of the lengthy digestion process of the cow which adds much beneficial bacteria to the substance. It is used in building the compost heaps as a starter and for its nitrogen content and in preparing the Biodynamic preparations.

Cosmic forces

Recognizing and working with the influences of heavenly bodies on plant growth by using the preparations and following the sowing calendar.

Biodynamic preparations

These simple, natural, homeopathic preparations are used to enhance the effects of the planets and of silica and lime on the soil and the plants, and also to enhance the breaking-down process and potential life forces in the compost heaps. Dr Steiner gave two preparations to be sprayed directly on the soil or the plants and six preparations to be used when making composts.

Crop rotation

Crop rotation, proper soil cultivation and other organic farming methods: intelligent planning to let the soil rest after heavy-feeding crops (such as potatoes, tomatoes, cabbage), by sowing green manures (legumes, clover) and covering the soil (grass, clover) so that it may build up its humus content and nitrogen levels; also mulching to improve soil structure, water and temperature balance in the soil, and to control weeds; companion planting to enhance growth and to control pests; using herbal tea sprays, special tree paste for fruit trees, creating raised beds, disturbing the soil as little as possible by shallow digging/ploughing and avoiding stepping on it or working it when wet, especially clay soils.

To deal with an unbalanced insect problem, animal pests or weed problem, one may collect the insects, weed seeds, or dead animal skins, burn them at the appropriate time according to planetary positions, potentize the ash in water as a homeopathic medicine, and spray it on the land. This is an effective biodynamic alternative to using chemical sprays.

The farm organism

The more self-sufficient a farm can be, the healthier it will be. The aim is to have a wide variety of plants and animals, and to bring something from outside (such as manure, bio-pesticides) only if there is an imbalance that must be rectified, as medicine. At the centre of the farm organism is the fanner, the human being who observes and has a close relationship to everything on the farm and who makes the decisions. Important aspects of the farm include the water source and balance, prevention of soil erosion by planting trees and hedges which also help in wind protection and providing animal habitat, being aware of insect life and balance which could include looking after honey bees. The farmer therefore is responsible for many beings and for fostering correct relationships, and is the temporary steward of the land, not the owner.

Weeds, Pests and Diseases

Weeds growing in specific places show a deficiency in the soil, as pests and diseases show a shortcoming in agricultural practices. They are signs for us to understand where the problem is, and actually help us to rectify imbalances. They are friends, not foes! It is well known and proven that insect pests and diseases will only attack weak plants, There by balancing the situation and stimulating us to be better farmers and gardeners.

Practical application

Walk around your land each day, become familiar with all its aspects: minerals, rocks present, type of soil, wild plants growing, types of weeds, insect life, animals present day or night, electric wires crossing over the land, underground streams, presence of water, weather patterns, people living on or using the land.

Establish environmental control: plant hedges and trees for wind protection, ensure good drainage, be aware of the water quality, use and collection.

Use mulching wherever possible; the Earth likes to be covered and will do it by itself with weeds! Build compost heaps and treat them with the preparations: do not waste any organic leftovers- collect everything. First compost manure and all other organic material, and apply only when completely broken down! It can be sieved to re-compost any under-com posted bits. Compost branches larger than your wrist separately as this will take much longer to break down.

Converting A Farm To Biodynamics
The important criterion is to sustain the fertility of a farm that lasts for future. The guidelines to be followed are;

All short term manuring use of water soluble fertilizers for quick growth is discontinued. This not only damages soil structure but also produces plants that are nutritionally unbalanced.

Stop all chemical weed control methods that will leave undesirable residues which inhibit the development of active soil life.

The type of stock carried in the farm is important as it has unique effect on soil fertility

Encourage legume growth, earthworm activity and other soil micro-organisms. This is enhanced by the biodynamic preparations. This brings about microbiological life to the soil and exerts a balancing effect on availability of minerals. They also influence the permanent build up of humus.

Need of adequate trees to provide shelter and shade as conservation of moisture, protection from wind and also act as predators.

Specific Biodynamic measures have now been in use for more than 65 years. Many farmers and gardeners know their effects from practical experience. Experimental evidence has also been produced, which has added to the available empirical knowledge. The measures include two groups of specifically fermented substances, which are called preparations. The first group includes 6 different herbal substances; they are numbered 502-507 and are added in small amounts to manures and composts. So they are collectively called as compost preparations. These numbers are arbitrary, having been chosen by those who first produced the preparations. The second group includes the sprays; they are numbered as 500 and 501. Although not considered one of the eight main preparations, a ninth preparation, sometimes referred to as 508 is made by boiling the horse tail plant and is applied only in excessively wet years to prevent fungal diseases.

BD 500 Cow horn manure

It is basically fermented cow dung. It is the basis for soil fertility and the renewal of degraded soils. It is buried in Sept./Nov and lifted in Feb/March. This is the period when the earth is breathing in and comic earth forces are most active (winter).

Cow horns, Fresh cow dung from a lactating cow.

Average 50-150 gms dung/horn (depends on horn size)

Feed cattle with high quality food for two days prior to collecting dung for BD 500 (good green fodder and less protein artificial feed).

Prepare burial pit: 18 inches deep. Pit area should not be subject to flooding, vigorous root systems or earthworms. BD 500 takes the character of the soil it is buried in, so good quality earth in the burial pit is essential.

Collect cow horns , remove any paint. Collect fresh dung –reasonably firm. Fill cow horns with cow dung in October/November (rather than September due to India's warmer climate). Place horns in burial pit, 1 inch apart with base downwards, surround with 50% compost and soil.

Cover with soil and bury for 4 to 6 months. If the soil is not rich enough, add compost to an extent of 50% to enhance soil quality. Keep burial pit soil moist and shaded, at temp of approx. 20oC and free from weeds and earthworms.

After 4 months check for dung fermentation. Dig up one horn. If the green cow dung has turned into a dark, smooth earthy smelling humus (BD 500) they are ready to be lifted. Remove the BD 500, use and store. If not, leave them longer.

Application process

- Apply when the dew is falling (the earth breathes in) i.e. late afternoon or evening – descending Moon.
- 25 grams BD 500/acre in 15 litres rain/pure warm water (approx. 15-20 °C)
- Check water for high calcium, iron or other minerals
- Stir for 1 hour alternately clockwise and anti-clockwise forming a vortex
- Spray in the late afternoon or evening (just before sunset), when Moon is descending

- Spray 4 times a year – during the beginning and after rains, i.e. Feb-May-Nov-Dec.

- Place in glazed earthenware pots with loose fitting lids.
- Bury in a box surrounded with coir pith, which is kept moist and can be closed.
- Keep in dark and at temp of not more than 25 °C.
- Use within 1 year.
- Effect/result
- Promotes root activity
- Stimulates/increases soil micro-life
- Regulates lime and nitrogen
- Helps to release trace elements
- Increases germination
- BD 501 Cow horn silica

This is finely ground quartz crystals specially prepared. The crystal should be of good quality, shape and clear. It is buried in a similar manner to preparation 500 but this time it is buried during the summer time (buried in

April/May and lifted in September). This is the period when the earth is breathing out and the cosmic light energy is most active (summer).

BD 502 Yarrow (Achillea millifolium)

This is made from yarrow flowers combined with the bladder of a stag.

Method of preparation

- Urinary bladder of the stag is used. The stag with its antlers magnifies the effect of the cosmos.
- Smell of the stag bladder and that of the yarrow are similar.
- Cosmos activity of the flower is enhanced by the cosmic activity of the bladder.
- The energies received by a stag from the cosmos through the antlers center around the bladder.
- Start the preparation making under the planetary influence of Venus.
- Blow up the bladder with air when the bladder is fresh.
- Air dry and then collapse.

- At the time of use moisten to make it flexible.

- Cut the bladder, insert a funnel and introduce the flowers till the bladder is packed.

- Moisten the flowers with plant extract, stitch up the slit with cotton thread.

- Store in a closed basket to keep away rodents/pests.

Time of burial to lifting

- Hang up in march to get cosmic influences
- Bury from September to March in a mud pot with earth inside

BD 503 Chamomile (Matricuria chamomilla)

This is composed of the flowers of the Chamomile plant combined with cow intestine.

Method of preparation

- Harvesting
- Pick flowers when petals are horizontal (mid morning-10 am)

- Ideal flower will have two rows of petals around the cone
- Harvest into a tray as the flowers if left together produce heat
- Use drying trays

In air tight containers.

- The intestine of a cow or bull can be used
- Do not wash intestine
- Cut into 15 cm bits
- Run finger along intestine, like milking a cow, to squeeze out undigested matter
- Tie cut bits at one end with a cotton string
- Fix funnel to open end and fill with dry flowers
- Pack not too hard or loose
- Stack the filled sausages into a bundle, which could be placed in a mud pot surrounded with fertile soil

Time of burial to lifting

- Bury in October and let it remain in the soil till Feb/March.

BD 504 Himalayan stinging nettle (Urtica parviflora)

Method of preparation

- Fill the dried leaves into terracotta pipes or mud pots
- Press well into the containers
- Ensure that the lid is on
- Place the pot under the influence of Mars
- (Moisten dry leaves with juice of leaves before filling if found dry)

Time of burial to lifting

- Harvest leaves in May and September
- Lift the preparation in September after a year

BD 505 Himalayan oak bark (Quercus glauca)

This is prepared by combining bark of the oak tree with the skull of an animal.

- Crush the oak bark

- The skull of any domestic animal may be used

The link between the skull and bark is their calcium properties. Further, it is the Ca formation and the skull formation that takes place first in the case of the development of the embryo.

- Place the crushed oak bark in the brain cavity of the skull. Block the opening with a well shaped bone piece.

- Place the skull in a watery environment with weeds and plant muck which would have been damaged by the local diseases that effect the crop. This helps buildup the resistance of the plants and follows the principles of Homeopathy.

- It should be placed in a location where there is exchange of water such as rain drain/swamp.

- It should be noted that a foul smell is emitted on lifting the preparation and removing it from the skull
- This gradually reduces with drying after removal in a dark dry place
- Fungus may form
- Turn over frequently to correct the same

Time of burial to lifting

The preparation is placed in September and lifted in March.

BD 506 Dandelion (Taraxicum officinalis)

It is made from the dandelion wrapped up in a bovine mesentery.

Method of preparation

Use the mesentery of the cow. The flower is very sensitive to light and hence it is placed in the mesentery of a cow, which itself is sensitive

- Ensure that extra fat is cut off

- Do not wash the mesentery
- Place the dried flowers in the mesentery and wrap into a parcel and tie with a jute thread
- Place the parcel in a good mixture of soil and compost into a pot

While lifting the preparation the mesentery may or may not be seen.

Time of burial to lifting

Place in September and lift in March.

BD 507 Valerian (Valeriana officinalis)

The juice of valerian flowers is used for this preparation.

Method of preparation
- Place the clipped flowers into a mortar and pestle and grind into a paste
- This paste is added to water in the ratio of 1:4 in a bottle
- Ensure storage in a cool place

- Use 1 gram each (502-506) for every 5 cubic metres of compost and 10 ml of 507 at 5% in 2-5 litres of water. These could be added to liquid manures and cow pat pits also.

Pits for burial of preparations

Size: Depth = 12-18 inches: Length = 2 feet; Breadth = 2 feet

Location: Fertile well drained soil with no trees in the vicinity (spreading of roots)

Maintenance

- Weed free. Dig trench around pit to prevent weeds/roots. Mulch on top with coconut pith
- Line the pit with bricks on the side but leave the bottom free
- A marker should be clearly visible (e.g. brick lining)

- Make a sign to define the preparation, date of burying and date of lifting, and a layout plan for our record
- Maintain pit temperatures between 25-30oC
- Maintain moistness by watering/sprinkling over the pits
- Water logging should be avoided

Choose a moist, cool, dark location with good air circulation

Place the ready preparations into well labeled glass jars or glazed pots

Place the pots into a well insulated storage box using e.g. coir pith

A food grade drum placed horizontal with a hinged opening is useful for preparations such as 500 and CPP

Turn the preparations frequently, and maintain moisture

BD 508 (Equisetum arvense)

It is very high in silica; it can be used as a tea to control fungus in the early season

It should be sprayed at full Moon (2-4 days before) and at Moon opposition Saturn, the same as BD 50

Materials

- 1 kg Equisetum arvense (Horsetail herb) or Casuarina
- 10 litres water

Preparation process

Make a strong tea/tincture by boiling the Equisetum arvense or Casuarinain hot water for 2 hrs. Let it sit for 2 days.

Application process

- Dilute the tincture: 50 grams tincture to 10 litres of water
- Spray onto the soil or over the plants in the early growing stages

- For mild fungus problems BD 508 is often sufficient, but for more severe problems BD 501 is more effective.

Conclusion

You can grow your own food using biodynamic practices, whether you have a small urban garden or room to spare in the country. Start with building healthy soil through composting, growing cover crops, and integrating animals such as earthworms, chickens, bees, rabbits, or goats, according to the space and type of land you have available. Increase your biodiversity by trying new varieties of annual and perennial vegetables, fruit, herbs, and flowers. Take your compost and soil to the next level by using the biodynamic preparations, which you can purchase from several local and national distributors. A precursor to organic farming, the biodynamic model relies on the interconnectedness of the earth and its inhabitants with the entire universe.

The goal is to create a self-sustaining farm or garden organism which unites plants, animals, soil, minerals, water, and other elements into interconnected balance and harmony to bring health to soil and produce abundant and nutritious food.

Biodynamic farming and gardening focuses on minimizing external inputs, and chemical fertilizers, herbicides, and pesticides are strictly avoided. Generating fertility and health from within the farm or garden is achieved through integrating plants and animals, composting, using cover crops, encouraging biodiversity, and using biodynamic preparations made from fermented herbs and minerals.

Planting and harvesting are guided by the movements of the sun, moon, and planets in relation to the stars and biodynamic farmers and gardeners work with their senses, listening to the land they steward and helping to bring it to its full potential.